Tears   Bottle

By

Nancy Routh

Copyright March 31, 2021

Nancy Routh

Director of

"In the Spirit Ministries"

An ACT International Ministry

ISBN 978-1-7372854-0-3

Table of Contents

Dedication & Acknowledgements

Jesus redeemed my life. I thank Pastor Bill Barnes for the guidance and relentless way he encouraged me to "Do something for Christ" in my early adult life. I am grateful for the powerful women in my life who taught me to intercede and pursue Jesus. I will forever thank God for the nurturing at Victory Fellowship where I discovered my calling. I thank God for my sister and brother; my mother, who despite her hard life, had a deep love for Jesus; my Father who gave me life; and my precious children—all three of them—as well as my dear grandchildren. I thank God for my clients and my current Pastors, Carl and LeAnn Albrecht.

Introduction

Isaiah 61:1

"The Spirit of the Sovereign Lord is on me, because the Lord has anointed me to proclaim good news to the poor. He has sent me to bind up the brokenhearted, to proclaim freedom for the captives and release from darkness for the prisoners,"(NIV)

I have worked with those who are downtrodden and wounded for many years. I was that person, too. Somehow, God turned ashes to beauty in my life, and in His patient and loving process, I became someone He designed me to be. I try to demonstrate the love God gave me and the compassion and the comfort of the Holy Spirit. Many on this earth are still walking in pain and suffering, and Jesus sets the captives free. I am an evangelist of a different kind. My ministry walls are prison halls, treatment centers and the streets—wherever there are people held captive. I am a seed planter and a waterer in Christ.

My children learned to expect my voice speaking by the Holy Spirit in my room as I endeavored to pray through a situation, heal my broken places, or enter into intercession on behalf of a client or friend. My life taught me a lot about my human limitations, but always, even when I didn't acknowledge God's presence, He was there for me. I have the faith today to trust in the one and only Trinity—the Father, the Son Jesus, and the Holy Spirit.

This book is my testimony to God's limitless goodness. No matter where I am, what pit I have fallen into, what life circumstance I am walking through, what healing I need, or what ministry he challenges me to, He is enough. Jesus loves me when my face is dirty. He loves me when I dust off, stand up, and move forward again. His love is greater for us than anything we can do, anything we can know. He desires a personal relationship with us even before we truly know Him, and He will always pursue the one. I pray that, as I share my story, you will understand through my transparency about my imperfect life, the height, the width, and the depth of His perfect love for you. May you find freedom from your past and know who God created you to be.

Chapter 1

The Beginning

I first knew Jesus when I sat on the front row in a Christian church. I was three, and I sat with my brother and sister who were told they were old enough to be baptized, but I supposedly wasn't. Before the pastor plunged them into the water, I clung to every word I heard and answered the same questions they did. When they went back into the water, I took a deep breath too and held it until they came up. My little heart was pounding, and I began to cry silently. My eyes filled with big round tears that forced their way out and down my cheek. I was so happy for my brother and sister, 'cause I felt it, too! I knew that Jesus had taken me to him and made me his. It was a revelation that I unconsciously carried through the torrid storms that plagued my life as I grew up on this earth.

I was born in a little Conoco oil town in northwest Kansas. Mama always told me my delivery was breach, but followed it quickly with, "It was the easiest labor, and even the doctors couldn't believe how easy it was." I reflected many times after having my own children, that it couldn't have been that "easy!" I was her Thanksgiving baby. She said it was the best Thanksgiving of her life! Some kids don't get to hear stuff like that from their mama. I think I always felt like a pretty special person, right from the beginning.

Mama had a way with kids. She loved every child she ever met, unless one of the kids picked on one of hers! I remember a picture she showed me of my brother and a girl that must have been a foot taller than him. Apparently, she became one child that Mama didn't like, because the story goes that the little girl bullied my brother. She told me that story each time we would look over the pictures for the next thirty years!

I know a lot about the earlier parts of my childhood more from pictures than from memory. The Brownie Camera got a workout, and Mom wrote on the back of many of the pictures so we could remember where we were and exactly what took place!

We lived in a little white farmhouse outside of a small oil refinery town. Daddy tried to be a farmer for a while. His dad was one, and he farmed their quarter 350 acres that they staked in the Homestead Act. I loved seein' my dad in that big ole' combine, rollin' through the fields of wheat. He seemed superhuman way up there in the cab. It was a John Deere, and daddy's name was John Wilbur. I think for a while I thought we owned the John Deere brand!

Turned out my uncle on daddy's side of the family owned a John Deere dealership, so it must've added to my confusion! Anyway, those wheat fields were so beautiful!

As I grew, my hair was long and straight and just the color of the wheat toast stalks that blew in the hot Kansas wind. The fields went on and on, mile after mile with barely any interruption of civilization. I embraced the beauty of the wheat against the sky. I could lie out there on my back for hours daydreaming in the wind, watching the clouds roll overhead. I learned early on the types of clouds and what they brought with them—rain, storms, trouble, or a simple peace.

It was a good thing I was taught early by the clouds that life could bring all those things. Somehow it was then and there I must have grasped that life could be good and bad, happy and sad, a struggle and painful and joyful—all at once, it seemed. It was shortly after that, that the simplicity of life changed. I have to say, that what I am about to share with you is harsh, but somehow, through all that I experienced in my life, I looked back and knew that Jesus had been there with me, right through the middle of every storm.

My mama and daddy got divorced, sometime during the year I was three. I didn't understand why for many years after that. Later on in life, I thought of two incidents leading up to it. My very first memory in life was of a black and white linoleum floor. Nobody took a picture of it, but that floor etched itself in my mind's eye, and was stored somewhere you put those things that are too painful. I was just under three years old, so it made sense that my toddler line-of-sight was the floor. I didn't really remember all what happened until I was 32 years old. It hurt too much, so by the grace of God, He hid the memory of it for me 'til I was older and could handle it through His love. When my memory finally allowed me to look up from that black and white floor, I was witnessing domestic violence. At the point of my healing, Jesus allowed me to see that I was not alone. He was with me on that floor; He had been weeping and holding me in His arms.

I recall one other incident; we were driving down a hot dusty stretch of Kansas road in our black Dodge. There were no seat belts in those days, and the dust blew up into our rolled down windows. I was daydreaming as usual when my mom must have opened the car door and, just like that, jumped out the car. We started screaming—my brother and sister and I— looking out of the back window as our precious mama rolled into the tumble weed ditch. That was the first time I thought I was losing her. Dad slowed down and pulled over and yelled to stay in the car as he walked back down the road. When the dust cleared our view, he was helping mama up out of the ditch. Some burrs and gravel had cut her up pretty badly. Her hair was tossed—that beautiful soft golden white hair I used to play with and twist around my fingers. I loved her so much and even so young, I knew that she was in pain—both inside and out. Daddy got her back in the car, and it was a silent stiff ride back to the farmhouse. After that, things changed even more.

After Mama and Daddy divorced, we moved to a little town in Kansas, Mama and my brother and sister and I. I liked our house, it was calm, and we had an upstairs! It was so much fun to run up and down those stairs and snuggle up in the attic room! We lived next to a wooded area that had some old farm equipment. My brother had a great comic book collection—Dick Tracey, Spiderman, The Blob, and many other superhero books! He made a fort at the top of an old combine, and we'd climb up there and read and laugh and share stories and play hide and seek for hours on end. My brother was big enough that he joined the boy scouts! I was so proud of him. Somehow mama had scraped enough together to buy him the whole uniform! He got badges and stood tall as he saluted, his hand touching the edge of his cap, just like he was in the infantry or something!

I got enrolled in kindergarten the year I turned four, and that helped mom, 'cause she didn't have to figure out what to do with me during the day. I thought I was pretty hot stuff, going off to school like my brother and sister. Oh, and talk about an experience! A little red head boy kissed me shortly after I started school! I wiped it off and ran the other way on the playground, but he liked me! I spent the rest of my days trying to avoid him!

One hot early evening, us kids were home alone as usual until mama could get off work. We had a piano in the house we rented, compliments of the owners; it was one of those big old uprights. We left the doors open so there would be a little hot wind circulating the house. We were too busy playing to hear the screen door open and close, but when my sister went into the dining room where the piano was, out popped a woman named Johnny that lived across the street with her parents. She grabbed my sister by the throat and proceeded to choke her. I screamed! I don't know where my brother was, but the struggle ensued. Luckily, Mama ran in the house from work, smacked the woman off my sister, and screamed at her to go home. Mama made sure Sue was okay, told us to lock the door behind her, and then stormed across the street, to Johnny's parents. My four foot seven inch mama was a pack of blazin' blonde hair, stompin' across that street, poundin' on their door, and told them what happened.

We never saw Johnny again, and Mama explained to us that she was not all there in her head and didn't really know what she was doing. I don't think she involved the police. As a matter of fact, that town may have been too small to have had a representative of the law! But Mama made sure that Johnny would never come around us again. I kinda felt sorry for Johnny, after what Mama told me. I don't know if I really processed the gravity of her condition, but something inside me felt sad for her. I wasn't conscious of it then, but now I know that was

God, softening my heart, makin' me feel the way He felt for her.

Daddy didn't come around much, but every few months, he might pull in and pick us up. He had taken up with a woman that must've been more sophisticated than Mama. She'd be there too when we had time with him, so I don't really recall having much alone time with my daddy after that. I was sure it hurt Mama, so it made me uncomfortable. We began a life that year of spending a week with Daddy in the summer and a few days at Christmas. I didn't understand 'til years later, that Mama probably gave up her Christmases with us, 'cause she knew we'd get real gifts from Dad and that side of the family. She didn't usually have much money for that. One of my favorite toys, though, was a doll she made us called ShinFu! Mama was so creative with things! I think she could summon up something out of nothing!

She started a tradition with us kids that year. Often at Christmas, my sister and I would share a gift, and my brother got something small. And each Easter she would give one of us a gift, rotating the years, telling us that our special Easter would come! We thought it was a great deal, cause most kids just got gifts on their birthdays and at Christmas! Easter was the other holiday that she loved because of Jesus. She'd take us to church, and we would have Easter bonnets and Easter egg hunts, with eggs that she let us help decorate! She always made things special.

Only one other thing sticks out in my mind from my kindergarten year. Living in Kansas, we had lots of tornado warnings, and people in Kansas don't mess around with tornados. We were taught early on that you hit the cellar and don't come out 'til it's all clear. When the town sirens started blaring, mama would grab her purse that always had her important papers in it, and we would get to grab one toy, and then hold hands and run to the cellar. It was one of those dug in the ground things with two doors that flapped down over the stairs that led us a few feet into the ground. Well on this day, mom had been making hamburgers. She remembered to turn off the stove, but my brother was not about ready to let the burger that had his name on it fly away in the funnel cloud! Sure enough, he headed back up those cellar stairs, slid the latch, and was plowing through the high wind to get to a burger...just like it was the Holy Grail and he was Indiana Jones.

In my memory, Mama is grabbin' at the doors that were swinging wildly in the wind, calling his name, and my sister and I are sobbing for our brother to get back where he'd be safe. The chaos began, screams became muted by the whoosh of the high wind, as we watched tree limbs and debris fly by. Sobs poured out in the deafening silence, and then above us stood my brother with the biggest grin on his face, holding his burger as if it were a medal of honor! My mother climbed up and yanked him into the cellar and latched the doors. We all sat there dumbfounded and relieved, and then just burst into the biggest chorus of laughter you ever heard! I think our bellies must have ached when we were finally able to stop. Silence surrounded us, but this time we weren't in the eye of the storm, the tornado had blown over and left us to journey on.

Psalm 107:29 "He stilled the storm to a whisper; the waves of the sea were hushed." (NIV)

Journal

When was your first moment you knew Jesus? Have you had that moment yet? If you haven't known Him, ask, "Jesus I don't know you, I don't know how to hear from you, but I know that I want something different in my life. Will you come into my heart?"

_____

_____

_____

_____

_____

_____

_____

_____

_____

_____

_____

Were your parents divorced? What was your
family life like? Write about some memories.

_____

_____

_____

_____

_____

_____

_____

_____

_____

_____

_____

_____

_____

_____

Reflect on your childhood. Write more about what you remember.

_____

_____

_____

_____

_____

_____

_____

_____

_____

_____

_____

_____

_____

_____

_____

_____

Prayer

Dear God,

I ask that you protect the hearts of those reading this book. As they walk through this journey, and memories re-enter their minds, take care of their spirits. Place someone around them who could be there if they really need to talk, and only allow what you know they can handle to surface. Scripture says, "I look to the mountains from where my help comes from." It comes from you, Jesus, from the comforter, your Holy Spirit. I know you can encompass those reading this book with your love, your compassion, and your peace. In Jesus I pray, tenderly hold and love these precious ones. Amen.

Chapter 2

The Journey

We did a lot of journeying! I think in the beginning, moving from town to town helped Mama deal with her unsettled spirit, but later, her travels took on new purpose. So, from place to place we went! Mostly we moved from one small town to another in Kansas. We would stop off at Grandpa and Grandma's almost every time between our moves. I realized as I grew, what a respite it was, to "be home." Their house was the only really consistent home I knew growing up. How grand it was to top the hill right before we got to town! Us three kids would always sit high in the car seat, so we could be the one to see town and yell, "first one to see Lincoln!" That was our game, every time we came back. It felt so good and familiar.

Grandpa and Grandma only lived in two houses all their adult lives, and never left that one town. Imagine that! One of the houses was a big house on the hill. When I went back as an adult, I realized it wasn't nearly as big as I remembered it as a kid! But ohhh the memories we made! Playing hide and seek, running around the yard, clacking at the chickens, and running for our lives when we knew Grandma was going to the back yard to swing a chicken around by its neck until it broke. Whew! But somehow it never bothered me when we had fried chicken that night. I am not sure if I put two and two together for a while!

The big house on the hill had a running stream of water going right through the dirt basement of the house. I was told that was "real special" and it apparently allowed Grandpa to heat the house with what they called steamed heat. We had big Christmas gatherings there, all our cousins and aunts and uncles came. It was so much fun. It was in those times that I felt like I belonged, that I had family that knew me. Mom still made sure we had Christmas with Dad, but he'd drive over and get us and take us to our other Grandma's house and then bring us back. Our time with him got shorter and shorter.

Well, my sister and I sat down one day when we were adults and said we were going to write down all the towns we had lived in. We were going to try to correlate it with the grade we were in, but neither one of us is sure that we ever got it all right. Memories got muddled with life. When Mom moved us, she always tried to make sure we made it through the school semester. That being said, it didn't always work out that way, and sometimes we even went somewhere different for the summer.

I remember one summer in particular. I think Mom was just trying to see another part of the United States. I heard people say she had some wanderlust. I wasn't sure what that meant then, but if she did dream of being an actress in Hollywood, so she may have also pictured herself being a world traveler! Anyway, one summer, we boarded a greyhound bus in Kansas, and went all over different states. Our memory doesn't serve us too well, but to the best of our ability, we remember mostly staying on the bus. Mom would unload us to grab something to eat, or stay somewhere long enough to get cleaned up, and then she'd plop us back on a bus! We went from town to town and state to state, oohhhing and aahhing out the window. We saw flashes of panoramic view, land and terrain we'd never seen before, cities too big to get off in, and glimpses of the people in their day-to-day lives across the north mid-west. We are not sure, like

I said before, but we think we went through Michigan, Iowa, Ohio, Illinois, maybe Nebraska and the Dakotas and who knows where else.

One memory I have from that period, was a monument we visited. It must have been in the Dakotas. I saw an American Indian man, in full native dress, doing a dance in the bottom of a concrete bowl. I became impressed by the movement, and sat on the side of the bowl, feet dangling over the side, but an overwhelming sadness hit my little spirit. I wanted to cry for him. I am not sure where my mom had gone, but I was there alone. When the man was finished dancing, he came over and sat right by me. We sat in silence for a minute as I awkwardly swung my legs back and forth. Then something welled up in my spirit, and I had the courage to ask him why they made him dance down in that bowl. He laughed and said, "Ahh, they think the tourists like it." My heart broke. Somehow, it spoke to me of an oppression I didn't really understand, but God knew that encounter had softened my heart. Once again, He was preparing my heart so I could have His heart—His compassion for all people.

It was always a relief though to land back in Grandpa and Grandma's arms at the end of our journeys. I think Mama felt that same sort of relief. The other house they lived in was a small little house on Lost Street. What a dichotomy! The only other place I knew as home was located on Lost Street! Now, Mama always did teach us "home is where the heart is," and I found that to be a truth. I am grateful to understand that it's the people, not just the place, that makes a home. That carried me through a lot of years of moving. The thing I loved about the little house is that it was the house my mama spent a great deal of her childhood in, although I can't imagine squeezing

Mama's siblings—three boys and two girls—in that little house.

I got to hear many stories about the hours she spent on the trapeze Grandpa hung for her in the back yard. She talked about spending her days out there, and eventually using rings. Her daddy, our grandpa, had run off from his home very young and joined the circus. I found out years later that his dad had been mean to him and beat him, so that's why he left so early. Anyway, he was able to teach my mama how to use the rings and trapeze! I always thought that was so exciting.

Mama's daddy became a barber once he and Grandma settled after they married. I have no idea if he really had any formal training or not, but it probably wasn't necessary when he first started. He had his barber shop with the barber pole right in the middle of downtown

Lincoln, so at some point he must have procured his license. I always took a lot of pride in knowing Grandpa was such a prominent businessman, and well respected by those in town. But I did fall prey to way too many pixie cuts as I grew up. Turn a bowl upside down on your head, cut around the bottom of the bowl and you've got a pixie cut! I think the haircuts were worth it though, 'cause I always got to take rides in the big ole barber chair! Grandpa would pump me up and down and spin me around. I loved that; it was another thing I could count on.

Like I said earlier, my daddy's dad was a farmer but became a big businessman in a neighboring little farm town. He was part owner of the Bank and a local store. He helped to run the little community and had originally settled there as a landowner. I think my dad had it rough growing up. I get the impression that

Grandpa was a tough man and demanded a lot from his boys. He may have even been one to really give out a hard lickin'. When dad and mom first got married, they lived at the farm with Grandpa and Grandma. They built an apartment onto their house for them. Grandpa wanted my dad to stay there and farm his land, but Mama and Grandma just didn't seem to get along. Mama was insecure and sensitive, I am sure, and Grandma had a tough exterior. Anyway, years later, when my dad was old, he reflected on their life at the family farm and said he thought maybe Mom and he could've made it, if he hadn't moved Mama in with his parents. I didn't have the heart to tell him that Mama had really loved somebody else all along. She had fallen in love with a piano player in high school who was killed in World War II. So, I doubt that their living anywhere else would've changed things, but thinking that probably helped Dad live with how life turned out.

My grandpa on Dad's side of the family, died before I was born in 1954, so I never knew him. Grandma had to liquidate property and businesses after the kids left home one by one, but she lived to be 99 years old. A few years before Grandma passed, she was elected the bi-centennial queen of Barnard, Kansas! I still have a picture of her all dressed up in her early 1900's outfit, holding a parasol. When I think of that grandma, I always remember her fresh blueberries and cream she served for breakfast at her house. I thought that was very fancy. The other thing I remember is something called Rocky Mountain Oysters. She made me eat one, one day, and I hated that thing...wouldn't even swallow it, just spit it out. To my horror, a couple weeks later one of my cousins laughingly told me what I had almost eaten. Let's just say, it may have taken most of my childhood to overcome that one!

Life was full of simple pleasure and old-fashioned experiences. We never had a lot of possessions, but I don't remember feeling like we were lacking anything. Most of the time, we had what we needed. Looking back, God provided.

Ezekiel 36:26 "I will give you a new heart and put a new spirit in you; I will remove from you your heart of stone and give you a heart of flesh."
(NIV)

Journal

Did you move a lot or stay in one place? How did
that affect you?

_____

_____

_____

_____

_____

_____

_____

_____

_____

_____

_____

_____

_____

_____

Can you think of a time God began changing your hardened heart?

_____

_____

_____

_____

_____

_____

_____

_____

_____

_____

_____

_____

_____

_____

Are there certain people you feel compassion
for? When do you remember first caring?

_____

_____

_____

_____

_____

_____

_____

_____

_____

_____

_____

_____

_____

_____

Prayer

Jesus, you designed this person with your special intent for their lives. You made them and had plans for this dear one before they were conceived in their mother's womb. I thank you for the amazing way you created each person. If things happened in their lives to attempt to cancel their destiny in you, Christ, I know you are the redeemer and will cause all your plans to come together. Help them to begin to see what they are meant to be in you, Jesus. Shower your love and peace over them as they seek you. Bring them to new understanding as they reflect upon what makes their heart break. Let them see beyond themselves into the world as you designed them to be. Amen

Chapter 3

Moving On

We would keep a few treasured items that made wherever we went feel like home. Mom'd buy new used furniture or rent furnished apartments when we went to a new town. Boy, Mama could put a house together really fast and pack one up just as quick! She was always happy setting up a new house and happy again when she set her sights on a new town. I think it was a way for her to deal with restlessness and to put creative change in her life. Before long though, we found out that the next town had something wrong with it too and the grass was gonna be greener on the other side.

I didn't mind being the new kid. New kids get a lot of attention, and I learned to fit in and make friends quickly. Looking back as an adult, I always had to leave them, but I gave it my all! It was easy for me to be friendly and be someone everyone liked. I usually was popular, but I always had a heart for the underdog. I think that was because I probably really felt like I didn't belong, and I knew what that was like! I can't for the life of me think where I lived in the first grade; maybe Sylvan Grove.

We had moved to Hays, Kansas for second grade and I did not like my teacher! Her name was Ms. McNutt, and I could say a few derogatory things about her name, believe you me! Have you ever heard of a second grader skipping school? Well, I did. About that time, we got our first black and white TV. I could watch cartoons and all 12 inches of the picture were amazing! Yep, I said 12 inches! Anyway, since I didn't like my teacher, it made perfect sense to sneak back home after my brother and sister turned the block to go to their school. We were latchkey kids, cause Mama had to work. I spent the day hanging out and watched cartoon after cartoon. There was even a soap opera on that I am sure Mama wouldn't have wanted me to watch, but I did.

Well the afternoon was going great until my brother walked in from school. I had lost track of time and forgot to devise a plan to make it look like I just came in from school. Hey, most second graders just don't think that far ahead! So, my big brother proceeded to plop me over his knee and give me a spanking like all get out! I cried and cried and when Mama got home had to tell her what I'd done. That pretty much cured me from skipping school. I might have pretended I was sick a few times, but never again did I really skip out.

Having to tell Mama the truth was a trait that was very alive in me. One time I lied to her about brushing my teeth and you woulda thought I robbed a bank! I tossed and turned that night in bed and sometime in the middle of the night got up and went into Mama crying and tellin' her I lied. She was gracious and responded with an equal intensity that I brought with my guilty conscious. Holy Spirit was alive and well in me even at that age, 'cause I couldn't live with myself lyin'! I'm glad lying was so hard for me. At some point not long after that, I think I decided I wasn't good at lying anyway and mainly told the truth from then on!

During that same school year, I tried to join the Brownie scouts. I got the Brownie hat and eventually the dress. Mama just couldn't get it all at once. Of course, when you join the Brownies, you have to learn the pledge. I don't know why, but I had some kinda mental block with the last part of it and could never memorize it right.

When we all said it together, I muddled through the words as if I knew it, but really didn't. It was a small town, and some of the girls and mothers weren't all that friendly. I knew I didn't have time for snobby people cause making friends had to happen really quick or we'd be moving again. One day the den mother told my mom if I wouldn't learn the rest of the pledge, I couldn't be a scout. I do remember having some hurt feelings about it but didn't really have time for that either. Needless to say, I had a short-lived stint with the celebrated organization of the Brownie scouts.

We made a few friends in the neighborhood though. There was a boy named Richard that really liked my sister Susan. We had so much fun making up backyard skits for anyone who would come. We'd hang a blanket across the clothesline for our stage backdrop and dressed for each role. At dusk on a summer's eve, we would play act into the night! It was quite dramatic, but it's a good thing there was no social media back then, because we even made Richard dress in drag. He had to play the mom in one of our skits. I am sure he wouldn't have done it except for the fact that he liked my sister that much!

During that same time, my brother had a crush on a pretty, dark-haired girl that I think was older than him. He didn't have much time for us, 'cause he was more interested in his girlfriend! Other than comin' home to eat, he spent his days at school and at her house, or off wandering.

We left town and went back to Grandma and Grandpa's for a little while that summer. I loved cuddling up in Grandma's feather bed. Why, you could sink into that bed like it was a cloud! The three of us kids laid crossways so we could all fit on the bed and positioned our heads so each of us could look out the window at the stars. A cool breeze would come in and we'd chat up the night 'til our eyes needed toothpicks to stay open. By five o'clock the next morning sounds would drift into our room from the kitchen. I remember hearing Grandpa and Grandma's hushed voices talkin' over the plans of the day as Grandma served him breakfast with coffee and sent him off to work with his sack lunch. Then I'd hear Grandma at the cutting board, rolling out biscuits or pie shells, pounding out meat for dinner, or cookin' bacon. My brother would hit the floor running to get a snack piece of bacon before Grandma put it on the table.

Mealtimes were really special at their house, and we never missed breakfast, lunch, or dinner! Breakfast was big and sometimes Grandma's surprise sticky buns made the whole house smell like cinnamon. She always had lunchmeat and chips for lunch, something we didn't get much of with Mama, and a major meat and three was always planned for the evening with some of Grandma's homemade yeast rolls. She would wait on Grandpa to get home, and then pull out all the stops. It was like he was the guest of honor every night of the week!

I loved watching them love each other. There was never a harsh word, at least not that we could hear, and he'd playfully walk up behind her and hug her when she was doing dishes, or when he thought nobody was lookin', he'd lightly smack her fanny. She'd always respond with an "Oh, pshaw!" which was the worst expletive Grandma ever uttered! That was her way of teasing him back. I never got to watch how a loving husband and wife should be with each other, except when I was with them. They spent all of 62 years in marriage and within just a few years of Grandpa passing, so did Grandma. I know she missed him like all get out.

Psalm 23:1&2 "The Lord is my shepherd, I lack nothing. He makes me lie down in green pastures, he leads me beside quiet waters," (NIV)

Journal

Did anyone in your life show you what a healthy relationship should be like? Think about what a good relationship should look like and write about it.

_____

_____

_____

_____

_____

_____

_____

_____

_____

_____

_____

_____

What memories do you have of your grandparents? What made you feel safe?

_____

_____

_____

_____

_____

_____

_____

_____

_____

_____

_____

_____

_____

_____

_____

Prayer

Jesus, help me to see the good that is coming out of my life. Help me to know the truth of my identity in you. Write about who God says you are. Look up scriptures that point to that.

_____

_____

_____

_____

_____

_____

_____

_____

_____

_____

_____

_____

_____

Chapter 4

Innocence Lost

This next year of our lives was probably the hardest. I know my sister and I couldn't remember a lot of what happened immediately after that year. Experts say when a child experiences trauma; the effects can stay with you through life. It is true. I also know that my God in Heaven and His son Jesus healed every part of me and my sister as we got older.

My third-grade year was the beginning of experiences that would make my sister and I feel different about ourselves and change our lives forever. We spent the year moving between Fort Collins, Colorado, the southern belt of California, and Yuma Arizona. The man mama met in Ft. Collins, Colorado, wooed her. The other thing he did was talk her into doing things away from the house, so he could "watch us." He had a sleazy friend, and I never did feel right around him. My brother couldn't stand either one of them. Sometime after my brother heard that mama was maybe gonna marry him, he called Dad and asked if he could go live with him. I'm glad he got to, cause no tellin' what woulda happened to him if he'd had to stay. I missed him so much though, and I know it was hard on him to leave us. He was just twelve and probably had a more normal existence with Dad.

So, Mom and Bob got married. He purchased the two of us Hollywood twin beds with white padded headboards. We thought they were beautiful, and up until then, my sister and I always had to share a bed. Little did I know at the time that he wanted to separate my sister and me so he could begin molesting her. I know God was with us, or we wouldn't have survived what came next, but it was years later when I went through some inner healing that I truly was able to see Jesus, carrying me and holding me, even in the darkest moments of abuse.

We were moved across country far from family or friends. We lived in the southern belt of California first, and my sister and I went to a Mexican mission school. I loved the open-air school, and the cafeteria fed us tacos and burritos for lunch. It was at this school that I saw some of the poorest of the poor right here in the United States of America. I remember going to the rest room one day, and a little girl was sobbing in the next stall. I asked her what was wrong, and she spoke out between the gasps of tears that her only pair of panties were so ripped that she couldn't pin them back together. I told her I would help, and we sat there on the floor in the restroom, as I wove the safety pin in and out of the soiled fabric and pinned her pants back together. It was at that moment in third grade, that God began softening my heart for those who had less. I wish I could have been her friend longer, but our stepdad decided we needed to move into Yuma, Arizona. First, we lived outside of town in something I would almost call a Quonset hut.

Migrant workers were the main population of that nothing town, and there was one general store. Later in life, I heard stories about the way the company store oppressed workers, by keeping them in constant debt, letting people borrow before they got paid and taking large percentages of their paychecks. It wouldn't surprise me if that was how that store was run. That knowledge fueled my indignation of oppression.

While we were in this town, I woke one morning to my stepdad whispering urgently,

"Climb out of bed, quick! Come to me. Don't move any more than you have to. Just jump and I'll catch you." I did as he said and turned back to see a scorpion shaking his tail in the middle of my mattress. It made me feel like I could trust him more, but that was a mistake. When I got older, and studied psychology and trauma, I realized that one way an abuser will woo his target, is to make things happen so they learn they can trust them. I often wondered if he had planted that scorpion in my bed. It wouldn't surprise me.

Shortly after that we moved into town. Now Yuma is very close to Los Algodones, and an easy walk into Mexico. I remember our stepdad taking us into town when mom was away at work. It felt bad, and of course later, realized that this grown man took us strolling through a town that was mainly for prostitution. I hated the way it felt with people gawking at us. When my sister and I grew up, we spoke about how he must have been trying to groom us to sell us into prostitution. It was in Yuma that he began to sexually assault me. I was still in third grade. My sister was already in such misery and pain, that when she heard him coming after me, she couldn't stand it. I will never forget how she loved me; she did for me what she did not have the strength to do for herself. It took a while, but we finally got Mom by ourselves to go out for pizza. My sister at the brave age of twelve was able to somehow tell Mama what had been happening, and with my sobs and nods, Mama believed us.

The next time our stepdad left the house, Mom grabbed some clothes and ran us out the door. I think back at how unbelievable it must have been for her to know that we went through what we went through, and how the man she thought loved her really just wanted her daughters. We were all broken. Mama drove without stopping all the way back to the safety of Grandpa and Grandma's. We let the wind pound us as we blew through town after town, stopping only to gas up and eat on the run, praying that it would all be left behind. Mama left us for a couple of weeks after that with Grandpa and Grandma. That was the second time I felt like I might have lost my Mama, but she came back and got us. She must've needed time on her own to grieve. To this day, I don't know where she went, and she never would talk about it.

Statistics say that by the time a girl is twelve in the United States of America, one in five girls have experienced some degree of sexual abuse. When I became an adult, I grew to know that Yuma, Arizona, is one of the hot spots in our nation for sex trafficking. I thank God every day that when that man paraded us through those towns, that the buyers must've thought we were too little or not experienced enough to take us at that time. My sister and I both shut the memory away for a number of years. I was twenty-three when I started having flashbacks of that atrocity in my life. My sister and I were two of the lucky ones; we got away.

Stunned, relieved or in denial, I really know what it means to see just one set of footprints in the sand. God carried us through the next years of life.

Jeremiah 30:17a "'But I will restore you to health and heal your wounds,' declares the Lord," (NIV)

Journal

What have you needed to heal from in your life?
What wounds do you still carry?

_____

_____

_____

_____

_____

_____

_____

_____

_____

_____

_____

_____

_____

When has God carried you through something?

_____

_____

_____

_____

_____

_____

_____

_____

_____

_____

_____

_____

_____

_____

_____

Beneath anger, there are feelings of hurt and pain. What are you angry about? Ask God to help with your anger.

_____

_____

_____

_____

_____

_____

_____

_____

_____

_____

_____

_____

_____

Prayer

Jesus, I know you can heal all things. Nothing is too big for you. You love me and don't want me to feel any shame or burden from the past. Lead me to your garden, Jesus—the one where I can sit by the river that flows from the throne in heaven—and comfort me. Let your refreshing waters pour over me and take away the weariness. I invite you to come into my heart and do heart surgery, Jesus. You are the healer, and all things have been bought and paid for by your birth, life, even your death on the cross, and by your resurrection. I praise you, Jesus! You have made me grateful for my life and your love. I am made new, in you. Amen.

Chapter 5

Wings of Refuge

It was the beginning of my fourth-grade year, and we moved to Oklahoma for a short time. It was hard and mom was really strapped for money. I remember waiting on her check one week and all we had was a package of soda crackers for two days. My sister wanted Mom to call Dad, but I think Mom was afraid he would try to take us from her, so she never would ask for extra help. One other time I remember Mom making a game outa eating potatoes. We had a bag of potatoes for at least 4 days. She said we were going to think of as many ways as we could to have potatoes. I can tell you... it was fun the first day; the second day it was a challenge; then the game just got really old. We had scalloped, baked, potato cakes, hash browns, boiled potatoes, and you get the idea. I don't know if they had food stamps in those days, but mama would have been too proud to ask for them anyway. We always made it through, but because of some of these circumstances, I had to overcome a "Poverty Mentality" in adulthood. I learned early on that Jesus would make sure we made it through, but I had to come to an understanding in my spirit that Father wanted me to have the best, and that I was not a child in poverty, but that I am a Princess in His Kingdom, and He wants me to have abundance in life.

We moved to Salina for the school year. Mama had read somewhere that music could help people who had traumatic experiences heal, so she scraped up the money to buy me a cello and my sister a viola. She made sure that we both started lessons, and I am sure that our instruments brought our spirits peace. Looking back on that, I think it is so remarkable that Mama knew that might be a path to healing. She never talked to us about what happened though. I guess she was hoping we would heal and forget it.

Not long into the school year, Mama got word that our brother had been thrown off a tractor and pinned under it and was in critical care. My sister and I must've stayed with our cousins; I don't really remember. She hired a little plane, which I am sure she didn't have money for, to fly to his bedside. Mama hated planes and hasn't been on one since, but it was necessary to get to Terry. I am pretty sure Mama prayed day and night, cause my brother did recover, and has a pin in his leg to this day. One tragedy after another kept hittin' our family. Looking back, I marvel at Mama's resiliency but know that each trauma took its toll—on all of us. The way God made the human spirit is amazing though. He protects hearts, and He never leaves us or forsakes us, even in our darkest hour.

God was definitely watching over my sister and me one day that year while we were still in Salina. We had gotten home after school and saw our stepdad's white van pull up in front of our house. My sister and I had learned to always lock the doors, so we hit the floor. We crawled on our bellies away from the windows, cause he was walking around the house peeking in. When we knew he had gone to the front of the house, we made our way to the back door, grabbed each other's hand and ran like crazy, all the way to Mama's work. Breathless and frightened, we told Mama he had come after us. She left her job right then and there, took us to Grandpa and Grandma's and started looking for the next place we could live. At some point she went back and got a few of our belongings, but for a few years, we all lived in fear of him finding us again. His trying to come after us was another confirmation in adult life, that he must've wanted us for sex trafficking. Thank you, Jesus, that you are our protector and that your wings of refuge are our hiding place.

That year we moved from Salina, KS, to Manhattan, KS; Lawrence, KS; and McPherson KS. I am pretty sure with each move that Mama was looking over her shoulder. She had managed to bring our instruments, so we were able to still play. She found someone at the college to give us lessons in Manhattan and Lawrence. During that time, a couple of people in Manhattan pointed out to me that I always held my head high, and that they thought I looked snobbish. I told them I was just a deep thinker, which was pretty true, but little did they know that if I let my head fall, I might not ever lift it back up. I had to hold my head high to survive and act like it was okay, when deep inside I hurt so bad and felt like I was dirty and worthless. That's what kids who experience sex abuse are left with. My remedy came later in life when I found out my true identity in God.

When we were in McPherson, one day after school my sister and I heard rattling at the back door, like someone was trying to get in. We don't know to this day if it was our abuser, but we ran to the front of the house, sat by the door holding hands, and told each other that if we saw him come through the back door we'd run out the front and if we saw him come through the front, we'd go out the back. I think hyper vigilance is the term I would know to use today, and paralysis. We were paralyzed by the fear of seeing him again.

Revelation 7:17 "For the Lamb at the center of the throne will be their shepherd; 'he will lead them to springs of living water.' 'And God will wipe away every tear from their eyes.'" (NIV)

Journal

Have you ever dealt with a "poverty mentality?"
How does that affect you?

_____

_____

_____

_____

_____

_____

_____

_____

_____

_____

_____

_____

_____

Did you ever have feelings of being less than or not good enough? Ask God to heal that.

_____

_____

_____

_____

_____

_____

_____

_____

_____

_____

_____

_____

_____

Has anything made you fearful? What?

_____

_____

_____

_____

_____

_____

_____

_____

_____

_____

_____

_____

_____

_____

Prayer

Jesus, please take away the fear. Anything that is stored in my body or spirit from the events of my life, I ask you to remove, and replace with your warmth and peace and love. I want to give any pain I have to you and ask you to carry this burden that I have carried so long in my life. I also ask that you help the protector in my spirit to look to you to realize that you are my strength and guard that will work together to keep me in peace. I don't have to go to the fight or flight place anymore. I can begin to turn to you, the living God within me, to help me overcome these feelings of unrest or anxiety. I trust in your love and will remind myself of that when things try to take away my peace. Amen.

I recommend you read these identity scriptures: Romans 8:28, 37; 2 Corinthians 5:17; John 15:15-16; Jeremiah 1:5; 1 Peter 2:9.

Chapter 6

He Poured out His spirit

After that, Mama moved us to Greeley, Colorado. It was my fifth-grade year. I remember walking two miles to school, carrying my cello. It was almost bigger than me, but I loved it. I got involved in dance that year too. I had some personal training from one of my teachers who was from Hawaii. She taught me Hawaiian dance and the language of the movement. I performed that year as a dancer for the first time in my life. I had found one more thing that could bring peace to my broken heart. I know that Holy Spirit was in that too.

Speaking of Holy Spirit, I usually walked to a nearby church and often would go by myself on Sunday. I don't know if Mama had gotten mad at God for what happened to us—she still did communion with us at home—but she stopped going to church. My guess is her shame was too great. In the early sixties, a single divorced woman was not always looked upon nicely, and now she carried the guilt of what happened to us.

I had found a small church just a few blocks from the house. Most of the churches I attended were probably Pentecostal or very active in the spirit. I know today that was God's plan! One Sunday I went up when they had the alter call. I remember hitting my knees and sobbing and asking God one more time to come into my heart. I knew something had changed, and as I stood at the door, shaking people's hands as they walked out, I was shaking on the inside, and from then on I didn't feel as alone or hurt quite as much.

That year in Greeley, I was asked to join the all-city orchestra. I am pretty sure that built my self-confidence, and I might have even puffed up a bit! Even though I had the last cello chair, I knew I was on my way to big things! I developed such a love for music and all the arts. Music, theater, poetry, and dance were what I imagined I would be involved in when I grew up. We even stayed in Greeley for part of sixth grade.

Mama met a really nice man that next year. He lived on a ranch in Carbondale, Colorado. It was a small town that was over the continental divide. She married him within the year. He wanted a family and especially kids 'cause he'd never had them. He was a really good man, and my sister and I felt protected. He cooked for us and helped us with homework. He'd make sure we got on the school bus standing knee deep in the snow. Some of the most fun times were when he'd saddle up the horses and take us horseback riding. He taught us to duck and weave in and out of trees, and how to choose a path that was best for the horse's footing.

Our house was heated by wood stoves, and I remember hitting the icy floor in the morning. Nine times outa ten he would have bacon or potatoes cranked up on the stove, and I'd throw some socks on so I could slide across the freezing floor to the warmth of the kitchen. My sister just kinda dealt with life and went through her days. She stayed to herself a lot. She liked having a dad she could maybe trust, but I think it was hard for her. There was never any talk of what we went through until we were older.

Like I said, we lived on a ranch. There was a main ranch house about ten acres away, and I had a friend who was my age! It was so nice to spend time with her after school. One day we took off on the horses and rode and rode all over the mountains. About four in the afternoon snow started falling, and within about one hour the ground was covered. When we looked around to get home, we were in a white out. A white out is when you're snow blind and can't see whether you need to go east or west. With the sun so far down and hidden behind gray clouds, we were lost. I remember turning this way and that trying to find something that looked familiar. We had gone too far to see the lights of either house.

It was cold and continued to storm. We were both getting panicked, and I remember I just started praying asking God to get us home. That kinda made my friend mad and frustrated. She thought she would get us home, 'cause after all it was her ranch! She'd grown up there all her life! I decided I still needed to put my trust in Jesus, and eventually we saw the dim lights of the big house. We were never so glad! We galloped all the way back.

Her parents had gotten real worried and her dad had gone down to get my stepdad, to start a search. Her mom fixed us a cup of hot cocoa, and in a while, they came barreling in the front door, full of exclamations and hugs and some scolding, but mostly relief! I will never forget how good it felt to be swept up and hugged by my stepdad. God's gotta have a special place in heaven for him, I know. I will treasure that moment forever. For a moment, I felt I belonged.

It was a couple months after that when Mom told us we were leaving. It made my sister and I really sad, we felt so safe there. But Mama had to do what she always did. I remember tearful goodbyes when he took us down the mountains. I thank God for him to this day. We moved to Laport, Colorado, then Loveland, and back to Greeley. Constantly on the move, I learned that Jesus would always move with me.

I went to junior high and my sister was in high school. Once again, we made quick friends. A few people remembered us from fifth and part of sixth grade. That was kinda nice and had never happened before in our lives! My sister reunited with a boy that had liked her when we lived in Greeley before. He became her high school sweetheart and they began being serious about each other. He was a persistent young man, one year older than her, and a couple of years later became the love of her life. They celebrated their 50th wedding anniversary this year.

During this year in Greeley, I remember a young man knocking on our door. He introduced himself and told me that he just wanted to meet me, that he had noticed me, and wished he could get to know me, 'cause he thought he was supposed to. He went on to say that his dad was a pastor, and he had to move again. I thought of that young man off and on in adulthood as failed relationships and years went by. I wondered if that had been the special one God had for me that I just missed. My sister was blessed with meeting her lifetime sweetheart, but I always wondered how I could have possibly met who God wanted for me with the town to town life we had. I always felt like I must've not been in the right place at the right time for him to bring me my love.

Life was good and felt familiar since we had lived in that town before. I was elected student council class secretary and was on the court for homecoming. It felt good to blend in for a while, just to be like other kids, instead of reeling in chaos and trauma. Mom had taught us to sew, and that always came in handy when the other girls could spend money for their dresses, I just went to the fabric store and bought some bright pink crepe fabric and made a sparkling belt to adorn my dress. I always felt proud that I had an original, and everyone always asked me where I got my dresses. I used to sew suit jackets and A-line skirts and even made my own bikini that year! There was no stopping me.

By the middle of my ninth-grade year, I was dating the running back and attending games, dances, hayrides, and get-togethers. My sister was working and buying her own shoes and clothes. Man, would I make her mad when she came in from school and saw that I had raided her wardrobe for something to wear to school that day! Mom made her share though, which only deepened her frustration with me! We were dressed in sixties bright oranges, lime greens, solids and flowers, compliments of my sister's job! I will never forget the day she came home, and I had her senior picture dress on. She was furious! I think I ran out of the house and stayed away until dark!

During those years, my sister and I had to make do with sharing a double bed again. We hated it! There were nights we had boot-scootin' bootie wars, shoving each other off "our" side of the bed. One night we got so desperate, we drug a plywood two-by-four outa the closet and stuck it in the middle of the bed, daring each other to cross it! Lookin' back, those were pretty laughable things considering the seriousness of our early life. It was nice to be concerned about such simple things.

My sister was in eleventh grade and in love. That year, she announced that she was pregnant and was going to get married and have a baby. Mom lost it! She was so angry she wouldn't sign the papers for her daughter to marry. That left my sister and her boyfriend with one alternative, so they borrowed his parent's car and drove to our dad's. Luckily, he signed the papers, and within a month I attended their wedding. His family had to take me because Mama wouldn't go. I never understood that. Shortly after, she announced that we were moving. I was old enough that I told her I wouldn't come, that my sister was having a baby, and she needed us. Mom said she would be leaving, but my sister's husband told me I could stay with them until the end of summer, and the baby was born.

I always marveled at how extraordinary that was of him, a young man just out of high school, willing to put food on the table for his precious young bride's sister. It couldn't have been easy for them to make it but make it they did! I got to hold and care for my sweet nephew after he was born until the summer was over. It was a tearful goodbye to my sister, and our bond is still so strong to this day. But Jesus stayed by her side in Greeley and helped her navigate caring for her new baby and her new life.

Psalm 126:5 "Those who sow with tears will reap with songs of joy." (NIV)

Journal

When have you been in a difficult or scary position and you had to put your trust in God?

_____

_____

_____

_____

_____

_____

_____

_____

_____

_____

_____

_____

_____

_____

What are you grateful for in your life?

_____

_____

_____

_____

_____

_____

_____

_____

_____

_____

_____

_____

_____

_____

Think back on your life. Who was there for you that you might not have noticed at the time? Was someone cheering you on, maybe even praying for you, even at a distance? Write about that.

_____

_____

_____

_____

_____

_____

_____

_____

_____

_____

_____

_____

_____

_____

Prayer

Father God, you have protected me and carried me through so many things. You have prepared my path when I had none. I am so grateful to you, Jesus, for the way you have guided me through, even when I didn't know you were there. You have placed people in my life to pray for me when I did not know they were praying. You brought them to speak a kind word to me when I had no human to lift me up. You narrowed the scope of my options, so I turned once again to you. You are patient and forever pursue my heart. It is true, you are my heart's desire, you and you alone. I turned to you and called out to you even before I had really seen the height, the width, and the depth of your love for me. You never, never gave up on me. You shaped me and molded me to become who you meant me to be. Amen.

Chapter 7

The Spiral

My sister had put aside the sadness of her youth and was moving on to make her own life. I think she remembered her trauma. I didn't much, or I shoved away the fragments that kept showing up. I had partially blocked it out of my memory only to rediscover the pain of my past later. High school years were fun, probably more normal than most of my life had been. We moved to a tiny town in Kansas. I tried out for cheerleading and made it, but my real passion was drama. I entered statewide poetry contests and tried out for plays. Somehow there was a depth of compassion in me that God had deposited, and it made me able to emote and put myself in other roles very easily.

That year I remember coming home from school and praying until mom would get home.

That was hours. I would pray that God would allow me to face the devil in my life and live for Jesus. Heaven knows why I would have prayed that at such a young age! Truth be told, I had already faced the devil, but I was sincere about serving God. I don't know why. It could have only come from Holy Spirit. I just wanted to live for God. Unfortunately, I didn't have a church home or guidance and it took a lot of my young adult years to plow through things of the world and get to what God had planned for me.

My eleventh-grade year I moved to Emporia, KS. I tried out for every play in school and usually got the leading role. I danced in the musicals and sang some. For the first time I felt like I knew who I was! I also was on the prom court, but as time went by, those things became less important to me. I was creative and that's what mattered, and I was still the champion of the underdog. God gave me a heart for those people who were excluded from the cliques—those people who may have been a little different and were extraordinary! Those people were my best friends.

When we first moved to Emporia, we lived in an apartment complex that the town people called sin city. That horrified my mom, and as soon as she could, we moved into a small house. While at sin city, I met kids from California that smoked pot and listened to Van Morrison. My exposure to things that weren't good for me had begun. It was the seventies after all.

My senior year, my high school sweetheart who had given me his class ring, moved to Emporia for college. He invited me to a fraternity party and that night, for the first time in my life, I drank. It tasted like Kool-Aid, and I began getting woozy. He helped me to lie down, and although I told him no, over and over again, he took advantage of me. That was it—the straw... the one that broke the camel's back. All this world's ways and the dissolution and sadness and emptiness hit me. The next morning, I went back to his college apartment, threw his class ring at him and screamed, "How could you?!" My heart was so wounded already, and then this.

I know now that I put myself in a compromised position, but I had trusted him and that was shattered—the pain cut deep. I had been so careful to abstain and then this was taken from me. Not only did I understand sex out of marriage was morally wrong, but I saw what happened to my sister when mom practically disowned her, and I wasn't about to fall prey to the same demise. This event ended my reasoning and rational thinking about relationships, and for a number of years, I acted out of pain and anger. I sunk further into revictimization of myself. Revictimization is when we continue to make choices that actually perpetuate our being victimized. It only makes our heart sicker and hurts us deeper in the long run.

I kept it together in school and had almost enough credits by the end of my junior year to graduate. Mom was against summer school and thought I shouldn't strike out on my own that young. After all, I started kindergarten so early and was just sixteen, so I stayed in school. My senior year, I made arrangements with the principal so that I would only have to attend three days per week. I told them my plan was to drive to Silver Dollar City in Branson, MO, and work four days out of the week. Since I only needed four credits to graduate, they went along with my plan. I auditioned and got a part in the theatre division and started my trips back and forth.

Mom and I lived near the college she worked at, so she walked back and forth to work, and I took her car four days out of the week to Branson. That was a huge sacrifice she made for me. Everyone I worked with was at least one to two years older than me, and by the summer I graduated, I began connecting with the creative kids that were experimenting with drugs. I moved to Branson on my own and a life of drugs, sex, and rock and roll allowed me to escape my past, for a while. My judgment was clouded, and I no longer thought the same way. In hindsight, I know God was there, but I stopped feeling like He was, because I turned away. I was riddled with my own sorrow and stuck inside of misery.

I became really good at acting like nothing was wrong, and self-medicated as much as possible. I am not going into a lot of detail about the next few years, but I had stopped even thinking about going to church. I muddled through my days, thinking that my creativity was being heighten by my various choices of substance, and I never had a thought that this wasn't how I should be. The devil was having a heyday, and I fell deeper and deeper into the chasm of numbed feelings and living a lie.

That next year I moved to Springfield, Missouri, and then Eureka Springs, Arkansas. I worked on a crew building a folk fair festival and met my first husband and the father of my children. He was a Nashville songwriter who came to play the festival. A mutual friend introduced us, and we were together from then on for a period of twenty years. Those years were riddled with his affairs and infidelity, and my heart was torn time and time again. Yet I stayed. Growing up how I did, I had no plumb line. I felt the affairs were wrong, but I was a victim still, so I remained a victim. I lived a lie so the pretense of having a family could exist.

Over the next few years, we travelled a lot, and often he travelled alone. We lived in Nashville, Arkansas, and travelled a folk fair circuit into Oklahoma, Arkansas, and sometimes into New Orleans. At one point, he was invited by Connie Stevens' band leader to go write and play in Las Vegas. I wasn't even of legal age to be in the casinos, so although we lived at the Flamingo Hilton where Ms. Stevens was working, I couldn't get a job. I spent some of my days playing with and teaching Ms. Stevens' daughters dance. A lot of people started saying I should audition for a dance part, and I eventually did. I did a lot of things I am not proud of, like taking my God-given talent of dancing, and choosing to dance in Vegas. I justified it to myself by saying, "It's choreography." Night life and living on the edge was my answer to the pain I didn't know would ever surface again. But pain always does, until you've dealt with it and healed.

Abuse manifests itself in so many ways. It does not have to be sexual. A child might have experienced neglect or witnessed domestic violence. Even a parent who is a workaholic and doesn't spend time with a child can leave a child with feelings like, "I am not valuable enough to spend time with." Various types of martial discipline or growing up in a household with a parent who uses drugs or alcohol can be abusive. Experiencing domestic violence and/or forced isolation are also forms of abuse.

Psalm 139:8 "If I go up to the heavens, you are there; if I make my bed in the depths, you are there." (NIV)

Journal

Have you experienced abuse or neglect in your life?

_____

_____

_____

_____

_____

_____

_____

_____

_____

_____

_____

_____

_____

_____

Have you allowed yourself to be revictimized in some way? Write about that.

_____

_____

_____

_____

_____

_____

_____

_____

_____

_____

_____

_____

_____

_____

What kind of behaviors did you accept for years that you can see now are self-defeating?

_____

_____

_____

_____

_____

_____

_____

_____

_____

_____

_____

_____

_____

_____

_____

_____

Prayer

Jesus, let me sit with you, and know you are next to me. I need your refuge. While I am here, I want to tell you how much you mean to me and how grateful I am for you. I am rich in you. There is nothing more necessary in my life, and you hold all of my wealth. I pursued things that were not of you, and yet you love me. You never deserted me or let me go. Every time I went away and came back, you were there. You are so faithful to those you love. Help me to be more like you. I want to be someone with your character and your compassion. Make me to know the width, the depth, and the height of your love. Remind me of who I am in you, and what I mean to you. Amen.

Chapter 8

The Lion's Den

The first time I spent time in New Orleans, I felt nauseous. I know now that was a spiritual warning, manifesting in the physical. I immediately wanted to go home to Nashville and could not stay longer than a couple of months. When it was announced we were going to move there permanently, I snapped to attention and dutifully followed my man into the Lion's Den.

My time there felt exciting in part. We renovated a couple of lofts to live in, and I connected with the New Orleans Ballet School. Although I worked in bars till two in the morning, I popped up at 8AM and took the streetcar to dance class. At one point I studied with a ballet Madame, who was talked into taking me on by my instructor. My technique improved along with my extension and my creative flow felt unstoppable. I became a pescatarian and worked long hours at my craft. At one point I was able to dance non-stop for 45 minutes, flowing through one jump to another, turning leaping, sustaining, and landing. My drug use had diminished to smoking pot on occasion and a little drinking.

I was able to study The Isadora Duncan Technique at Loyola University with a second-generation daughter. Isadora never had children of her own, so she called her students her daughters. I had the privilege of helping with the opening of the Contemporary Arts Center in New Orleans and was one of the first dancers to perform there—both solo and in a small group. A philanthropist and real estate dealer gave me a space on Decatur Street for a dance studio. At one point I had guests who included a member of the Alvin Ailey dance troupe and other modern dance groups touring the country at the time. Things felt like I was actually in sync. Weekend fishing trips to the bayou were a regular occurrence and getting to know the Cajuns that lived in the area was delightful.

But New Orleans can be a very dark city. Voodoo and sin shaped the corridors of the Vieux Carre, along with street people, wheelers and dealers, bikers, and mafia. I lived in a shadow of lust and debauchery, manipulation and deceit. I remember my man coming in one day and saying he was going to play for the Hell's Angels that evening. I am so grateful I didn't get invited or go. They came by in a van that evening. Later, he told the story of having a hood put over his head so he couldn't see where he was going. He entertained at their brawl and was dropped back off the next morning, having worn a hood on the way back into town, sworn to secrecy forever.

I will share one more story about my time there. Another couple encouraged us to take a trip with them. We toured the northern Midwest. Collecting song material was the motive for the adventure. The couple we were with decided to stay on the road, and when we returned to New Orleans, we were asked to have audience before one of the mob bosses. I was so naive. Apparently, the couple we travelled with had stolen a huge amount from a club owner, and since we were with them, they thought we were involved. We were asked in to talk one at a time, I guess to see if our stories matched. I heard something in my spirit say, "Just tell the truth." I am living proof that God continues to be there for us even if we have stepped away.

When I was called in, the door I entered closed behind me. I turned when I heard the door close and realized I couldn't see the door.

There was no knob, and the wallpaper was seamed perfectly, so it was as if there wasn't a door. I was motioned into a medieval-looking chair, with a high back and wide arms. I focused on the man sitting in the only other chair, a man I recognized as being a very powerful man in the Vieux Carre. Then my eye caught some movement in the back center of the room. Before me was a black panther, pacing back and forth on what looked to be a huge cushioned lounging area.

The man asked me if I knew why I was there, and after a "no" shake of my head, he proceeded to question me about missing money and the other couple and where I thought they were, and what we did. Apparently, what I said satisfied him, because after a long pause he said, "You can go." He pushed a button on the arm of his chair, and the wall became a door again and he gestured for me to leave. I knew that day I had been in a real lion's den and I often wondered if he had another button or one command that could have released that panther to his prey. When I look back at my twenties, I know God had his hand on me even then, and that day He truly delivered from the lion's den.

I struggled for years, trying to feel better. I didn't even realize what I was doing. I tried one drug after another attempting to plunge my re-emerging memories and flashbacks into the depths of my consciousness. I really didn't like the effects the drugs had on me, so I would give that one up in lieu of trying another. This experimentation went on for about ten years. Finally, I met my match. Cocaine was the one drug that could give me a euphoric high like no other. My cocaine addiction lasted for a chaotic three-year period. At first it was occasional use, and then soon became daily. Meanwhile, I was leading such a dichotomy of lifestyle. I practiced healthy eating and by then, vegetarianism, and was up nearly every morning by 8, headed to the dance studio to study and workout. That only helped me justify my use, but something about the way dance kept me connected to my spirit, probably helped me survive. I thought that I still had my life together, but I was addicted, broken, and wounded emotionally.

We moved back to Nashville and lived with a music manager for the next year, who was also a dealer. Every night when the drugs ran out, I would try to put myself to sleep, crying out to God in my spirit to deliver me. That cycle continued through the third year, until I had prayed myself to sleep enough in my sickness, that Jesus miraculously gave me courage to leave. I told the man who would be the father of my children that I was moving out. He could come with me if he wanted or stay, but I was getting out, and we had to stop using.

Psalm 69:1-2 "Save me, O God, for the waters have come up to my neck. I sink in the miry depths, where there is no foothold. I have come into the deep waters; the floods engulf me." (NIV)

Journal

Have you had an experience with Jesus, where you know He loved you despite your visible situation?

_____

_____

_____

_____

_____

_____

_____

_____

_____

_____

_____

_____

_____

Can you think of a time when God was there, but you didn't realize it?

_____

_____

_____

_____

_____

_____

_____

_____

_____

_____

_____

_____

_____

_____

Ask Jesus for forgiveness of things in your past. Then know that it is done.

_____

_____

_____

_____

_____

_____

_____

_____

_____

_____

_____

_____

_____

_____

_____

Prayer

Jesus, I know that you died for all things I have done. You took them on the cross and when you died, all sins were forgiven. Not part of them, no exceptions—*all* things were forgiven. Jesus, I cannot thank you enough. You paid a huge price for me and I have lived my life in ways that I am not proud of. That is my past, and today, Jesus, I ask you to help me leave that in my past. I have your word that I am forgiven, and that is enough for me. If I catch myself trying to pick up the blame, I will ask that my thoughts be your thoughts. I will call those old voices that want to keep putting me down a lie and remind myself I am a new creation in you. Thank you. I want a deeper, personal relationship with you. Amen

Chapter 9

Out of Darkness into Light

Through the next years, God blessed me greatly. I got pregnant and had my first child the year after I quit using drugs. I began going to church again and was baptized in water this time, when my oldest son was three. I found a career in communications that took me professionally beyond anywhere I had hoped or dreamed! God provided for us. I taught dance as an artist in residence at Vanderbilt that summer, choreographed some music videos, and some churches began allowing me to do some liturgical dance. Jesus was turning ashes to beauty in my life. For a short while, my husband began writing some songs that were more God-focused and we did some work for United Methodist Publishing. My pastor at that time continually told me, "You've got to do something for God, Nancy!" That was Pastor Bill Barnes. A man who stood up in his life for the oppressed, instrumental in the civil rights movement. He was also one of the founding pastors of the agency I later worked for, helping people transition from prison to the world.

When people stop using drugs, emotions flood into your spirit, and memories resurface. I began some inner healing work and started my healing journey, because after my first son was born, I was bound and determined I didn't want to carry my dysfunction into my children's lives. I am sure I did, especially when it came to codependency, but I was a work in progress!

My husband's addiction got worse and worse, after bouts of trying to quit, he continued use. It drastically changed the man I had deeply loved. I was emotionally abused, put down and eventually the abuse turned to domestic violence. I prayed and stayed much longer than

I should have, as most women do who are in the cycle of domestic abuse. Eventually because of something my precious stepdaughter said to me, I woke up. My eyes were opened, and I could see the truth.

Once again in my life, I was one of the lucky ones that got away. I say that, not really believing in luck, but in the divine intervention of my God. It is estimated that more than 10 million people in the US are domestically abused. 1-in-3 women and 1-in-4 men have experienced some form of domestic violence by a partner. Many of those relationships end in homicide. FBI data from the mid-70's to mid-80's demonstrated that for every 100 men who killed their wives, 75 women killed their husbands.

When a child is physically or sexually abused, we have potential, if there is no intervention or counseling, to continue to choose unhealthy people. My youngest son was just two weeks old when, one violent night, I had the courage to have my husband arrested. I went back to work a week later with my black eyes, and renal surgery that restructured my deviated septum. The people that God put in my life during this recovery are forever etched into my heart. I worked at the time for Kenny Roger's promoter. I have never known such generous and caring people. They allowed me to bring my newborn to work with me. We set up a nursery in the kitchen, and the amazing women I worked with took turns with me, holding my infant throughout the day. He was probably held and cuddled more than if I had him at home! My eldest son was in elementary school by that time, and we had some incredible neighbors that helped with after-school care. To this day, I am so thankful that God put these women and men in my path, and that my boss had such great compassion.

I truly believe God delivered me from my drug addiction. My healing journey was one of prayer, self-help books and individual secular and Christian counseling. I began understanding addiction and codependency. Eventually, as a single mom, I practiced nightly compartmentalization—a technique I teach my clients to this day. I learned to pull out my anger, pain, and sorrow, in the limited time I had to myself after my children were in bed. I began journaling or rolled up in a ball on the floor in a fetal position, rocking myself for comfort, crying to God to take the pain, and thanking him for my deliverance. When eleven o'clock hit, I would put my precious emotions in an imaginary box and go to sleep so I could get up the next day, be whole to love my children, and go to work.

My relationship with God grew, as did my beautiful children. I saw that my children were raised in Christ and promised myself that I wouldn't move a lot but would stay in or around Nashville so my children would have that stability of knowing home. I was attending a Holy Spirit-filled Pentecostal church and had been praying for my calling and purpose in Christ, when one day I heard in my spirit that I would go into the prisons! After arguing with God for a little while, I told my pastor. He told me there weren't really any positions in their prison ministry at the time. Unknown to us, the women who had been doing prison ministry, after many faithful years of service, wanted to step down. Within two weeks, the woman had spoken to the pastor, and he contacted me. When God intends for something to happen, He will always make the way. The Lord put me in the Tennessee Prison for Women as a pulpit minister and that began my life of walking His walk for His people, meeting them right where their needs are.

The irony of God sending me to a place where women were held captive did not escape me! I had been a prisoner, and captive all my life to the lies of the enemy. I battled low self-esteem and struggled with always feeling like I wasn't good enough. But God's love is sufficient, and He healed me.

Isaiah 61:1 says "The Spirit of the Sovereign Lord is on me, because the Lord has anointed me to proclaim good news to the poor. He has sent me to bind up the brokenhearted, to proclaim freedom for the captives and release from darkness for the prisoners," This became one of my life scriptures. The second one is in Isaiah 54:16-17. It says "'See, it is I who created the blacksmith who fans the coals into flame and forges a weapon fit for its work. And it is I who have created the destroyer to wreak havoc; no weapon forged against you will prevail, and you will refute every tongue that accuses you. This is the heritage of the servants of the Lord, and this is their vindication from me,' declares the Lord." Not a day goes by that I don't experience the presence of my Savior, my deliverer, my strong tower. He has been with me in some difficult moments in the prisons, and yet He tamed the lions and closed their mouths and caused them to sit down. I found most people were like me, hurt and wounded from life's hardships.

That was twenty-five years ago. I laid down my career in film and advertising which no longer satisfied the longing in my spirit to see people set free. Since then, I have worked on a daily basis in the mission field with people coming out of prison, the homeless, the wounded, and the addicted—men and women who have suffered trauma, neglect and abuse. They are people who the world would say are "less than," but God has given me His eyes to see, and they are the jewels of His Kingdom. They are precious sons and daughters of my God most high... just like me. That is what he created me to be. He took all my tears I cried and is now pouring them out because I am His vessel.

Jesus knows your sorrow and pain, even if you don't yet know Him. If you have had trauma, abuse, or neglect in your life, he wants you to know who you are in Him. He is the good Father. I had trouble seeing Father for a while because of the abuse I experienced from males. Jesus was my go-to, and the Holy Spirit, but gradually I found a way to accept my Father in Heaven. Through my relationship with Abba Daddy, I have been able to heal and then forgive my earthly stepfather and father. I got to have a relationship with my birth dad as an adult, and I know that he acted out of his own woundedness as did my mother.

Jesus is the Savior of the world, He was born of a virgin, lived on this earth and walked among us, he was crucified and raised from the dead on the third day, and He sits at the right hand of my Father in Heaven. He is in me, and I am in Him. He said I will go where He goes and do all these things and more!

My Savior is a loving advocate for all His children. He is the God that tends over any injustices in our lives. Today, in my work with my precious clients, Jesus and I are collecting tears in a bottle.

Psalm 56:8 "You number my wanderings; Put my tears into Your bottle; Are they not in Your book?" (NKJV)

Journal

Think about the next steps you want to take. Write about that.

_____

_____

_____

_____

_____

_____

_____

_____

_____

_____

_____

_____

_____

_____

Who do you wish you could say something to?
Write them a letter but know that it will be
healing just to write it. Before you send it, ask
why you are sending it. If your letter is harmful
to someone else, you may not need to mail it.

_____

_____

_____

_____

_____

_____

_____

_____

_____

_____

_____

_____

Prayer

Dear God,

Let your word be the healing balm of Gilead to my wounded spirit. You promised you would uphold me with your right hand. Help me through these times. Help me to seek you so I can find all the abundance of life you promised. Your scriptures said that you were sent to set the captives free. I believe that you can release me from the things that bind me. Help me to counteract the self-defeating words I hear with your truth. May the words I speak be life-giving words. Please send the Holy Spirit to comfort me in this time of healing. Lead me beside still waters and restore my soul. I acknowledge that I have a life to lead with you and for you. You are my strength and strong tower. Amen.

Chapter 10

Grace

My sweet mama lived out her ninety-two years, never disclosing some of her pain and sorrow. When she was very old, I told her one day that God had let me remember what I had seen that day as a three-year-old on the kitchen floor. I knew why she had to leave and understood. I think it gave her spirit some peace.

Mama finished her days, not involving another man in our lives. I saw her sitting with her big white bible on her lap in her room, underlining verse after verse. She knew the love of God, and although she told me one time she couldn't go to church anymore because when she went, she just cried, I knew that the Holy Spirit was in her—her comforter—and that she loved Jesus. Mama also deeply loved her children and grandchildren.

Jesus redeemed what the locusts had eaten, and my dad and I were able to have an adult relationship. I never told him what I had seen. That was one of those times I had to evaluate whether telling him would do more harm than good. It was clear to me that was the past, and it would serve no good purpose to mention it. He never knew to say he was sorry. He just became a different person through the years. In the end, I remember asking him if he knew who he was to Christ, if he knew what he meant to God. He shook his head and said, "I don't suppose so." I told him that day who he is to His good Father, his Father in heaven. I believe he accepted that. It was good to love my Father.

Jesus first loved us, so much so, that he died to take on our sins. I forgave my abuser, knowing that some human taught him what made him sick. I thank you Jesus that you gave me your gift of compassion, to forgive those who can't help themselves. Holding onto hate and pain only makes the heart sick. I chose to let go.

Now I am free through Jesus Christ.

John 8:36 "So if the Son sets you free, you will be free indeed." (NIV)

In the Spirit Ministries

"Building up the body of Christ in the fullness of God's Kingdom by sharing testimony and the truth of our sonship, authority and life in the Holy Spirit. Encouraging deep personal relationship with Father, Son and Holy Spirit."

inthespiritministriesact@gmail.com

My desire is to have a copy of this book available to women in prison, treatment centers and domestic violence shelters.

May God heal them as he did me.

To Donate

https://actintl.givingfuel.com/in-the-spirit-ministries

Make checks payable to: In the spirit ministries/ACT Int'l

Mail to: ACT P.O. Box 1649 Brentwood, TN 37024-1649

Made in the USA
Monee, IL
10 September 2021